ZULU
HERITAGE OF A NATION

ZULU
HERITAGE OF A NATION

AUBREY ELLIOTT

Struik Publishers (Pty) Ltd
(a member of The Struik Publishing Group (Pty) Ltd)
Cornelis Struik House
80 McKenzie Street
Cape Town 8001

Reg. No.: 54/00965/07

First published 1991
Second edition 1993
Second impression 1996

Text © Aubrey Elliott
Photographs © Aubrey Elliot except:
p 5, p 7 ABOVE and TOP, and pp 12/13 © Protea Hotels

All rights reserved. No part of this publication may be reproduced, stored in a retrieval system or transmitted in any form or by any means, electronic, mechanical, photocopying, recording or otherwise, without the prior written permission of the copyright owners.

Designer: Joan Sutton
DTP setting by Struik DTP
Reproduction by Unifoto (Pty) Ltd, Cape Town
Printed and bound by Kyodo Printing Co (Singapore) Pte Ltd

ISBN 1 86825 179 9

FRONTISPIECE *The regalia – in particular the head dress – of this young lady shows her to be of marriageable age. The dress of girls of pre-marriageable and marriageable age varies among the clans of the Zulu, and such factors as combination of bead colours used can have a specific significance. The umbrella, used even in clear weather on ceremonial occasions, adds a finishing touch.*

PREVIOUS PAGES *This typical Zulu kraal is situated in a rugged area of KwaZulu. Interpreted literally, KwaZulu means 'The place of the Zulu'. The layout of the huts in this home indicates that the man has a number of wives.*

OPPOSITE *Two young Zulu males practice the art of stick fighting. This form of 'relaxation' is not only a rugged sport, but also an exercise in the art of self defence. Cracked skulls are a not uncommon result of these jousts.*

INTRODUCTION

Historians have traced the beginnings of the Zulu nation to the late 1600s, when a man named Malandela (possibly a member of the Gumede clan) and his wife, Nozinja, are said to have lived a nomadic life in the Babanango area of Natal's northern midlands. In their wanderings in search of grazing for their cattle and better hunting grounds, Malandela and Nozinja eventually came upon an area of Natal where they discovered the picturesque Mandawe Hill, which lies a few kilometres outside the present-day town of Eshowe. They chose to settle on the west side of the hill, and indeed it was an ideal spot, as the hill overlooks the lower ground through which the road to Nkwalini and Melmoth now runs.

It was probably not the grandeur that decided Malandela to make his new home here, but rather the fact that the site gave him an excellent view of the fields where his cattle grazed and enabled him to spot the game roaming the area. His cattle and the game supplied his family with milk, meat and skins for blankets and wraps.

The shelters in which these old people lived were primitive forerunners of the beautiful thatched rondavels seen today. As the seasons changed and the climate varied, so it was inevitable that new grazing had to be sought from time to time, and thus it was impractical to build any form of permanent dwelling. Some protection from heat and rain was needed, however, so cone-shaped structures of sticks were built and covered with grass and sometimes animal skins.

Legend has it that old Malandela was not long spared to enjoy his hillside home at Mandawe before he 'went back home' to join his ancestors. The religion of the Zulu, and indeed of all the Nguni peoples, is one of ancestor

ABOVE *Visitors to a Zulu home must formally approach from the cattle-byre entrance. The cattle byre is the central point of any kraal, because it is a 'place frequented by the spirits'. The wives have their respective huts on the left- or right-hand side of the byre, according to the order of marriage.*

RIGHT *The rugged Valley of a Thousand Hills is home to many Zulu people. Parts of it are so inaccessible, that the residents use donkeys to transport themselves to trading stores.*

worship, based on the belief that when a person dies, he or she will continue to watch over his or her people from the spiritual world.

The Zulu have a saying: 'According to the power and authority a forefather had in his lifetime, so it is from the place to which he has gone.' This in effect means that a person carries into the next world the influence that he had during his lifetime. The spirit of a Zulu king will watch over the whole Zulu nation, for example, while the ancestral spirits of a family will care for that family, as well as their cattle, goats and crops.

The ancestral spirits 'like to be remembered', and offerings will be made to them to show that they have not been forgotten. At family festivals it is usual for the head of the family to sit beside his cattle byre and pour a little beer on the ground 'for his fathers' before he himself starts to drink. A woman may take a small piece of bread and place it under the eaves of the hut for an old matriarch of the family. If the ancestors are forgotten, they may show their displeasure by visiting some misfortune on the family.

Although the religion of the Zulu is centred on an ancestor cult, they nevertheless believe implicitly in a god, Nkulunkulu ('the Greatest of the Great'). Nkulunkulu will, however, involve himself only in major issues – matters of life and death. He is believed to be the creator of everything, and from this stems the belief that 'man is born healthy'. As they say, if 'He who made all things' made man, how could it be otherwise? Because of this belief, the Zulu cannot accept that accidents or disasters apart from very minor ones are natural phenomena. How can there be any malfunction in a perfect world in which all things were made faultlessly by Nkulunkulu? If such a malfunction does occur therefore, the people concerned believe that someone is trying to do them harm.

After Malandela's death a rift developed in his family, and Nozinja decided to emigrate to the north, taking her son, Zulu, and her loyal man-servant Mpungose with her. Her eldest son, Qwabe, did not accompany them; it is said that he had quarrelled with his mother over her small herd of white cattle, of which he was supposedly envious.

Up north the trio ultimately settled among the people of the Gwabini clan at a spot between the White and Black Umfolozi rivers, which today is an area dotted with many Zulu historical sites. Both Nozinja and Mpungose belonged to the Gwabini clan and were, by tribal law, in fact considered 'brother and sister'.

As the little household belonged to a patriarchal society, Zulu became its head, for a woman (in this case his mother) is, in Zulu society, considered to be subservient to the senior man in the family. This should not, however, be interpreted as suggesting that a woman of strong character will allow herself to be dictated to – far from it – but her accepted role is that of running of her household and training her daughters. 'Men's affairs are men's affairs', a Zulu will say.

In due course it became time for Zulu to take a wife, and his mother found the lobolo or 'bride price' to be given to the bride's father from her little herd of white cattle. The custom of lobola, that is handing over cattle to the father of the bride as compensation for the 'loss' of his daughter, is still common to all the black peoples of southern Africa. The number of cattle so

ABOVE *Sorghum beer is offered to one of the visitors to Shakaland for him to taste and approve. Thereafter the rest of the guests may partake of the beverage.*

TOP *Shakaland, run by the Protea Hotels group, is one of the more popular tourist resorts offering a traditional Zulu experience.*

ABOVE *A Zulu craft stall displays its wares alongside a highway in Natal. Sales of pottery and other items are brisk at these venues.*

TOP *Blood River is named after a battle that took place between the Boer leader Andries Pretorius and Dingaan's Zulu impis. The Zulu were defeated and the name of the river came about because the waters were said to have run red with Zulu blood.*

handed over for a prospective bride will depend on her marriageability, and a suitor could give upwards of 20 cattle for the daughter of a chief or a girl of similar social standing, while the average family could ask for four or five animals. Sometimes the consideration handed over may also include other livestock such as a horse, household items such as pots and pans or blankets, or any other items on which the parties might agree – the variations are governed by circumstances. The arrangements are made between the families of the prospective spouses, and a girl might in fact not even know she is about to be married.

Of interest is the fact that despite the migration of rural blacks to suburban townships in modern times, the custom of lobola has not disappeared but continues in these areas just as it does in the country. It is so firmly rooted in black society and so greatly valued for the protection it offers the bride that it is almost certain to remain as an important social custom for the forseeable future.

In the townships it is usually not a viable proposition to pay the lobolo in cattle, so the amount is set in rands. The average rate is R400, though much more will be handed over for a particularly eligible bride. In deciding lobolo in the townships, much emphasis is placed on the degree of education of the prospective bride.

The marriage of Zulu and his bride marked the beginning of the Zulu clan, and it also laid the foundations for what was to become the Zulu nation. To this day the Zulu lineage constitutes the royal house among the nation's numerous clans. Since Malandela the realm has had some 15 rulers, including the present king, Zwelethini Goodwill.

Little is known of Zulu's life, or those of his successors – Punga, Mageba, Ndaba and Jama. Towards the end of the 18th century, however, Jama was succeeded by Senzangakona, who became involved in an 'illicit' love affair with a young girl by the name of Nandi. Around 1787 Nandi bore the chief a son, and named him Shaka.

Young Shaka's childhood was not happy; he and Nandi were banished by Senzangakona, and mother and child were left to make a living as best they could – a situation which is thought to have had a profound influence on Shaka's character. The hardships he endured while roaming the veld in search of food and shelter almost certainly imbued him with the character that contributed to his aggressive attitude and affinity for the battlefield, and produced the ingenuity and drive he showed while building his formidable force of Zulu warriors. It is said that Chief Dingiswayo of the neighbouring Mtetwa saw early on the promise in this young man and coached him in the ways of soldiering and leadership.

When Senzangakona died, his favourite son, Sigujana, quietly assumed the mantle of chief of the Zulu clan. This did not suit Shaka at all, so he set about making plans to dispose of Sigujana. Shaka enlisted the help of Gwade, his half brother, and together with some accomplices they plotted to waylay Sigujana one day as he went to the river to wash. Thus Sigujana's life was ended after a short reign, and Shaka left no doubt as to who would take his place, in spite of the fact that Dingane, another of Shaka's half brothers, jealously opposed him.

Shaka soon built up a powerful army of warriors, arming them with his ingenious invention the short-handled stabbing spear, which replaced the throwing spear used previously, as well as a club with which to fight to the death. Shaka placed great store on physical fitness, and his impis were trained in rough terrain, without footwear, in order to become hardy, fleet of foot and disciplined even in the most rigorous conditions.

At the time of Shaka's ascent to kingship (1816), a number of strong tribes were emerging in the area that later became known as Zululand. Among them were the Ndwandwe under their wily leader Zwide. A clash between Zwide and Shaka was inevitable, the more so when Zwide brutally killed King Dingiswayo of the Mtetwa. Many battles were fought before the Ndwandwe were defeated and the small Zulu clan became the most powerful black nation on the southern African subcontinent.

It was at the now famous battle of Qokli Hill (1819) that Shaka won his greatest victory through brilliant military strategy, even though he was afterwards left with a badly depleted fighting force. Shaka positioned himself on top of the hill and thus gained a clear view of his surroundings – for the duration of the two-day battle he was able to see every move the enemy made. The hill was also some distance from the nearest water, and this meant that large numbers of the Ndwandwe were continually forced to break off from the battle to find water to quench their thirst. The Zulus, on the other hand, had made proper preparations: large stores of water and food were placed on top of the hill for the use of their warriors.

Shaka was severely outnumbered, with only 5 000 men fighting the 12 000 Ndwandwe, and even though he managed to reduce the odds by sending out a herd of cattle as a decoy, he remained at a considerable numerical disadvantage. The leader of the Ndwandwe, Zwide's son Nomahlanjana (Zwide himself had decided to remain at home), at one point drew up his lines and charged them up the hill, but the closer the warriors came to the top, the more crowded together they became. Eventually they did not even have enough room to throw their spears. The Zulu then charged down the hill and easily beat the enemy back.

The following day Nomahlanjana sent a broad column of men straight up the hill, like a battering ram aimed at Shaka. The Zulu king replied with his classic 'buffalo horns' movement: two columns of Zulu (the 'horns') ran down either side of the Ndwandwe column, while the main force met it head on. The 'horns' then closed around the Ndwandwe, completely encircling them and destroying the entire column.

Shaka then made a crucial mistake by splitting up his forces in order to search out any remaining Nwandwe warriors. The small contingent he took with himself ran headlong into a large enemy force returning from chasing his decoy cattle, and only the timely arrival of relief forces saved him.

Perhaps one of the most remarkable features of this battle was that amongst the combatants were five of the most notable and intrepid trailblazers in the history of the black nations of southern Africa, each of whom had an important influence on the lives and destinies of his people. Firstly there was Shaka, towering over his Zulu and forging a new nation out of a clan. On the opposite side was Soshangane, who escaped with a

ABOVE *This crocodile with a fish in its mouth was carved by a 14-year-old boy living in the Tugela mouth area.*

TOP *This splendid head dress for a bride comes from the Cele clanspeople in the Port Shepstone area.*

ABOVE *King Zwelithini Goodwill KaCyprian Bhekuzulu is a direct descendant of the first leader of the clan, Zulu, and is the 14th ruler of a dynasty dating back to the late 17th century.*

TOP *The mace of the Legislative Assembly of KwaZulu is made of gold, silver, ivory and ebony. It was created by engraver Percy Cave, who completed it in 1973.*

remnant of Zwide's vanquished army and eventually made his way north into Mozambique. Here he went on the rampage and finally achieved fame as the founder of the Shangane nation, whose kingdom stretched from north of Maputo to the banks of the Zambezi River. Fighting in the ranks of the Zulu alongside Shaka was Mzilikazi, who later broke away from Shaka, took a band of Zulu warriors with him and swept through areas of the Transvaal, Orange Free State and Botswana. Gathering momentum as he went, he ended up in Zimbabwe where he built his kraal at Bulawayo and founded the Matabele nation, whose territory ultimately stretched beyond present-day Harare. There was also Shaka's successor, his surly, brooding, jealous half brother Dingane, who later killed the Boer pioneer Piet Retief and his group of men. Lastly there was Mpande, Shaka's half brother by yet another of old Senzangakona's many wives. Mpande eventually helped the Boers overthrow Dingane and himself took the Zulu throne, giving his people 30 years of peace and a great heir named Cetshwayo.

It was the warriors of this same Cetshwayo who 60 years later (1879), made headlines around the world when they routed over 1 000 of Lord Chelmsford's British redcoats and allied forces in an hour and a half at the battle of Isandlwana and silenced every gun before racing on through rugged hills to Rorke's Drift, 14 kilometres away, where they engaged the British defending the border post there. This second battle was also an epic; of the small garrison that managed to hold the Zulu at bay for 12 hours that night, 11 won the Victoria Cross for their gallantry. Neither before nor since has this number been equalled in a single battle.

Cetshwayo's forces were finally defeated by the British at Ulundi, his capital. Ulundi was burnt to the ground, and Zululand was divided into 13 fragments, before being annexed by Britain in 1887. It was finally incorporated into Natal ten years later. The military might of the Zulu had been destroyed, and apart from the so-called Bambata Rebellion of 1906, which was swiftly and ruthlessly crushed, was never to rise again.

The Zulu nation today has a population of some 5 300 000 (1985 census), making it the largest of South Africa's black population groups by quite some way. The nation's king is Zwelithini Goodwill KaCyprian Bhekuzulu, and his chief minister is Mangosuthu Buthelezi.

I had the privilege of attending the induction of King Goodwill in 1971, and regard the occasion as perhaps the most impressive ceremony of its kind I could ever hope to see. The loyalty and enthusiasm of the multitude of subjects attending the two-day ceremony was overwhelming. The formal South African Government ceremony was followed the next day by the tribal Zulu induction, and I was privileged to witness the latter from within the sacred precincts of the royal cattle byre itself.

Part of the ritual involved the 'offering up' of a full-grown black bull, which had to be caught and killed by young Zulu men – barehanded, without a spear, knife or implement of any kind. Shortly before the event, the rain (a good omen) had poured down in torrents and the byre was a quagmire. Half a dozen muscular young males wearing only loincloths worked their way through the mud in the byre and picked a young bull from among the other cattle. The animal seemed to sense trouble, and fought furiously from the start, but in the end was overcome by sheer weight of numbers, its neck broken.

The bull was skinned in the byre and prepared for the feast, at which everyone celebrated the ascension of their new king, whom they refer to as *Ngonyama* and *Ndlovu*, the Lion and the Elephant – both animals being symbolic of the king's power and his strength.

The Zulu people today are a far cry from the war-like nation of the last century that attracted world-wide attention through its wars with the white settlers of southern Africa. Many of them have become urbanized, and follow callings in many walks of city life. Although the traditional customs and beliefs of the Zulu are still strongly upheld in the rural areas, and to some extent in urban areas as well, they are rapidly being eroded and replaced by the dominant Western culture of South Africa. It is only a matter of time, therefore, before an important part of South Africa's cultural heritage becomes something of the past.

ABOVE *The shield and spear are reminders of the days when the Zulu were a warrior nation. This flimsy spear is actually a throwing spear, and would have been used largely for hunting.*

LEFT *The splendid regalia of the rickshaw operators can be seen in Durban. The lightly-built, man-powered conveyances were introduced to South Africa in the 1890s, and were originally purely functional. With growing competition, however, the Zulu pullers adopted increasingly decorative styles of dress to attract the attention of customers.*

ABOVE *This fine old gentleman is one of the Cele clan in the south of Natal. The huts of his six wives can be seen in the background.*

LEFT *This man is dancing at a religious ceremony at Ekuphakumeni in KwaZulu. Spontaneous dancing among tribespeople is common, being an expression of happiness or appreciation.*

PREVIOUS PAGES *The leopard-skin chest and head pieces of this well-dressed Zulu man signify royal blood in the wearer.*

ABOVE *These two 'warriors' are beautifully dressed in full regalia. Although the warlike days of the Zulu are long gone, spears and shields are still carried at ceremonial occasions.*

RIGHT *Two 'warriors' of the King's Royal Household give a demonstration of their skill in the art of dancing – an integral part of Zulu public life.*

ABOVE *The style of a woman's head dress is usually determined to a degree by the clan within the Zulu nation to which she belongs. This one comes from the Dundee area, not far from the historic battlefields of Isandlwana and Rorke's Drift.*

LEFT *This married woman of the Ncunu clan sports a detachable head dress, made of a mixture of her natural hair and a coarse knitting wool. Head dresses from natural hair are not uncommon, though they are often somewhat smaller than the one pictured here.*

RIGHT *The elaborate beadwork head dress of this lady signifies that she is a diviner. The beads are strung in loops because, the diviners say, ' ... the spirits we call up come and sit on these loops of beads and speak into our ears'. Her heavy, pleated ox-leather skirt is typical of the style worn by senior Zulu women. These skirts are usually made by the men for their wives.*

LEFT *Diviners often choose to identify themselves specifically. The red bow worn by the woman on the left is for this purpose. Her companion is of the Ntombela clan, and her head piece and belt are examples of the originality of that clan's beadwork.*

BELOW *This beautifully beaded young girl is of the Cele clan in the Port Shepstone area. The small dancing staff is peculiar to this area.*

ABOVE *The splendid beadwork of this girl of the Cele clan in southern Natal shows her to be of a marriageable age. The custom of dying half the hair red is a popular local custom, not a 'universal' Zulu practice.*

ABOVE RIGHT *This woman is the senior wife of a much-married man. The wives dress almost identically, and the juniors have to be particularly careful not to outshine their elders.*

RIGHT *A uniformity in the style of dress in a given area is normal among tribespeople. If a person oversteps the accepted dress codes, he or she runs the risk of being accused of boasting.*

Marriageable girls of the Ntombela clan set out to join up with a party of dancers of the same age group for a Sunday afternoon's dancing.

ABOVE *Three young girls chatter outside the door of a traditional hut, while enjoying the sun at Shakaland near Eshowe.*

LEFT *This photograph of a young girl was taken in the 1970's at the Pobana Trading Store some 20 kilometres from Eshowe. The store was run by Kingsly and Gill Holgate. who later began the popular tourist attraction of Shakaland.*

LEFT *Two girls in the foothills of the Drakensberg mountains make their way to a nearby trading store to 'buy more beads'. Their outfits are particularly original examples of Zulu beadwork.*

BELOW *The womenfolk of most of South Africa's tribal peoples have a love of colour, and Zulu girls are no exception. Whether it be in beads, cloth or brass, they thoroughly enjoy decorating themselves.*

LEFT *A young Zulu maiden looks out over the Valley of a Thousand Hills, given a golden hue by the rays of the rising sun.*

BELOW *Proud mothers everywhere love to decorate their little girls, and the Zulu do not differ in this regard.*

The traditional Zulu beehive hut is built using exclusively natural materials, and comprises a framework of saplings thatched with plaited grass or river rushes. The thatching, a skill for which the Zulu are justly famous, is done by women. The end result is a sturdy, neatly constructed dwelling which will provide shelter from sun, wind and rain.

ABOVE *The Zulu people have an amazing ability to adapt to circumstances. The mud-plastered stone wall shown in this photograph is of a home in a residential area where termites abounded and thatch and wattles were not only scarce, but impractical. The look on the little boy's face is caused by fear of the camera. The wooden block behind him is a head rest (not recommended for comfort), while the large stone is used for grinding corn.*

ABOVE RIGHT *Two Zulu men construct the framework for a new wattle and thatch hut. The saplings are tied together with rushes, before the frame is thatched.*

LEFT *The door of the Zulu hut is woven from wattle. It is pulled across the doorway at night to keep domestic animals out.*

ABOVE *Cattle are treasured among the Zulu, not only for the products they yield, but because they are used as lobolo in marriage. The cattle are kept in a byre at night, and taken out to graze during the day. The tending of livestock in the veld is very much the chore of the young boys of a homestead.*

LEFT *The wooden stamping block is an indispensible item in the traditional Zulu household, as it is used for crushing maize. Once the maize is crushed it is boiled and eaten with sour milk – a dish they call* isitambu. *The grinding stone is used to make meal from both maize and sorghum.*

ABOVE *The women of the household attend to the cooking – usually the elder daughters help the mother. Cast-iron pots are popular cooking vessels.*

RIGHT *A group of young girls stop their daily chores to chat awhile. The erect posture of Zulu women allows them to carry almost anything on their heads.*

39

ABOVE *Men of the Cele clan gather over a pot of home-brewed beer. The old diviner seated at the back, with inflated goats' gall bladders on his head, was the proud husband of six wives.*

RIGHT *Smoking is a popular form of relaxation among the Zulu, although they are not generally heavy smokers.*

41

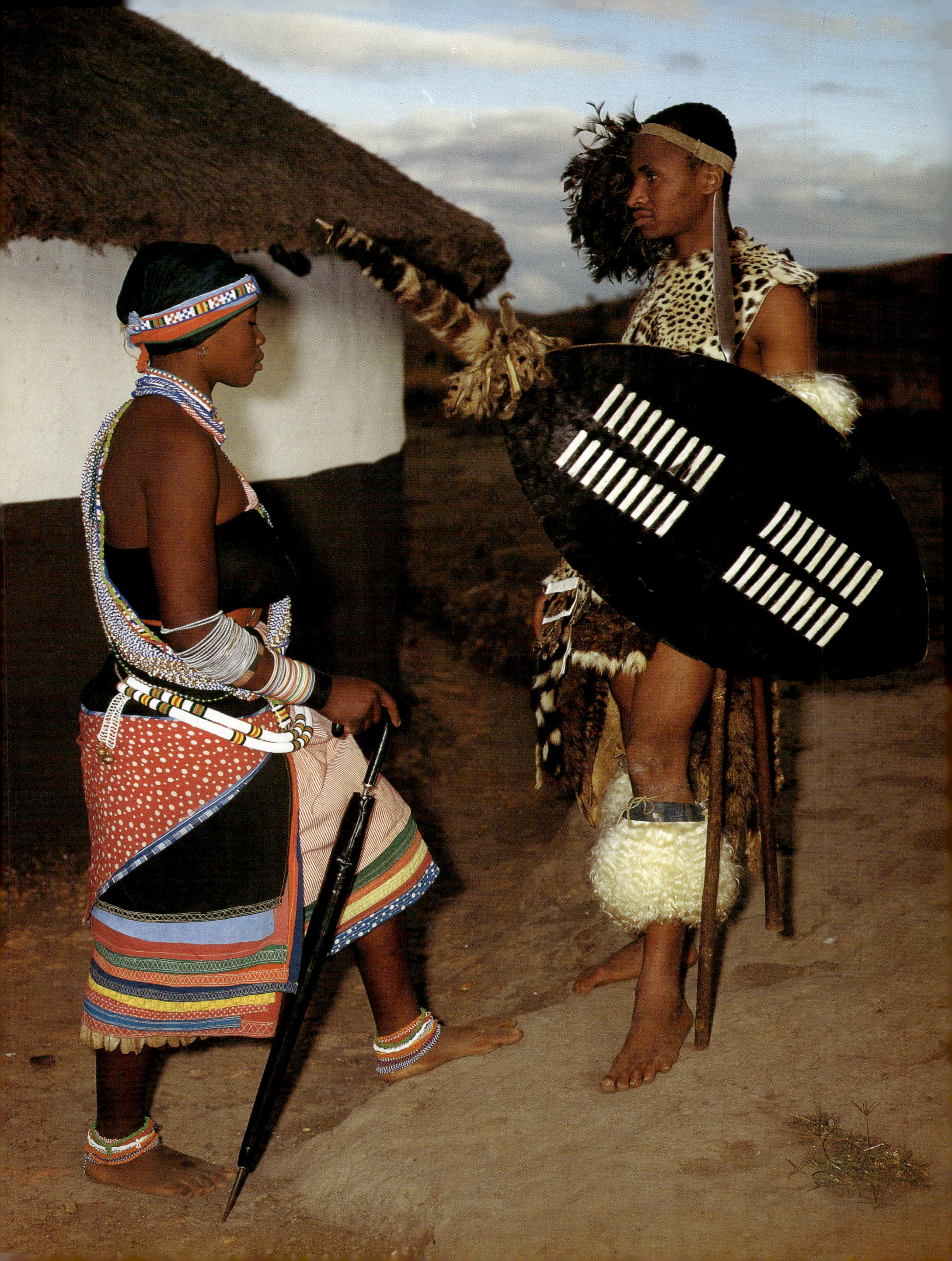

LEFT *A young couple of the Cele clan in southern Natal meet for a chat at dusk. Even today, Zulu men will carry their shield and spear as part of their formal going-out regalia. The women, for their part, are particularly partial to a black umbrella as part of their formal regalia.*

BELOW *Dress often varies noticeably from area to area within KwaZulu. This young couple are from the rugged Tugela Ferry area, quite some way to the north of the Cele clanspeople.*

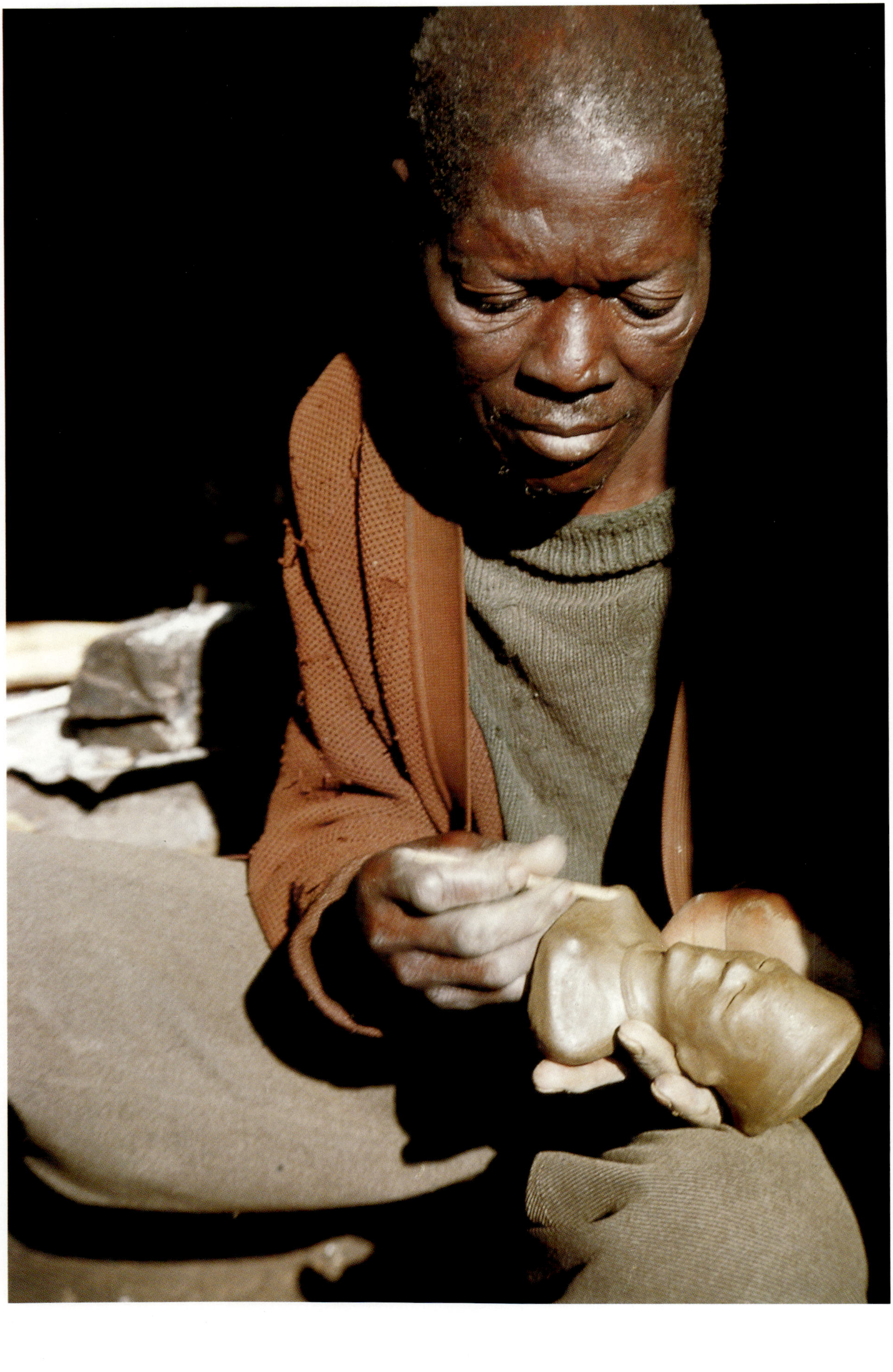

ABOVE AND RIGHT *Ma Mpungose is a potter who has earned herself a considerable reputation. The clay, taken from the same quarries as that used by the potters of Shaka Zulu's day, is kneaded on a stone slab, before the base is fashioned and placed in a circle of grass (called an* **inkhata**) *to steady it. The sides are then built and rounded, patterned, and finally polished with a smooth stone.*

LEFT *While the Zulu are prolific producers of clay pots for their own uses and for sale, they are not, to any great extent, sculptors. Hezekiel Ntulu was an exception, however, and he earned himself a fine reputation, particularly in Natal. Among the students he left behind him was James Nzuza, seen here sculpting a head out of clay.*

ABOVE AND RIGHT *Once the pot has been shaped, it is baked in a fire. The leaves of an aloe are used to make this fire, as they burn with a very intense heat. Once the pot has been fired, it is enclosed in a heap of dry grass, and blackened in a fast-burning, smoky fire.*

TOP *This giant pot, made by Ma Mpungose, weighs 22½ kilograms, and was baked under a large truckload of aloe leaves. In the making, it was propped up on the inside with stakes to prevent it from collapsing.*

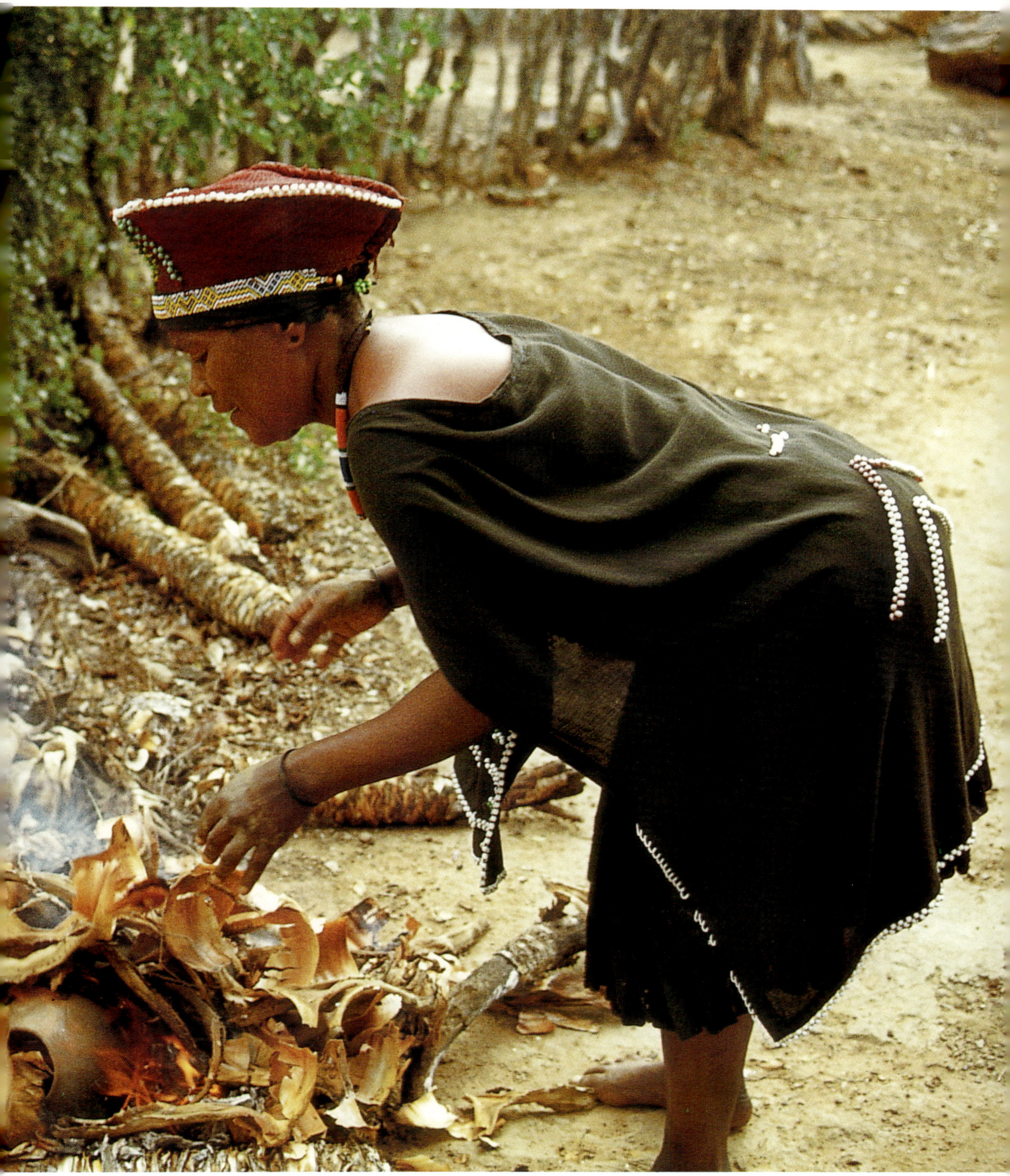

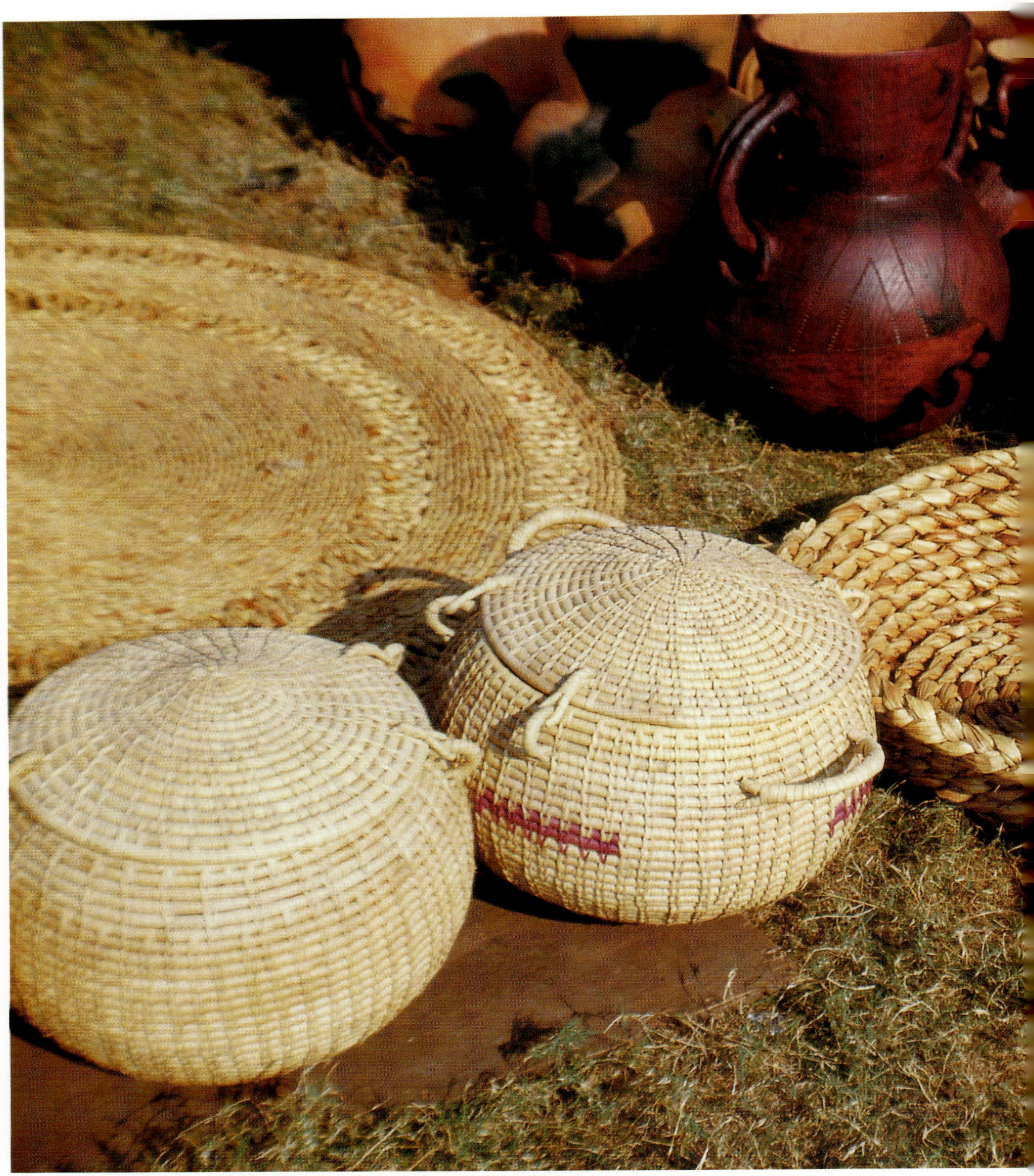

The motoring tourist to Natal and KwaZulu will find many wayside stalls selling works of art in the form of pottery and leather or basket work. While many pieces may be conventional in style, often much initiative is apparent in the pieces offered.

ABOVE *Zulu water pots are specifically designed so that their contents will not spill when they are carried.*

ABOVE LEFT *The design of these pots is not a traditional one, and is probably copied from the designs of the china flower vases often found in Western homes.*

RIGHT *Baskets are woven both for practical domestic use, and for sale to tourists.*

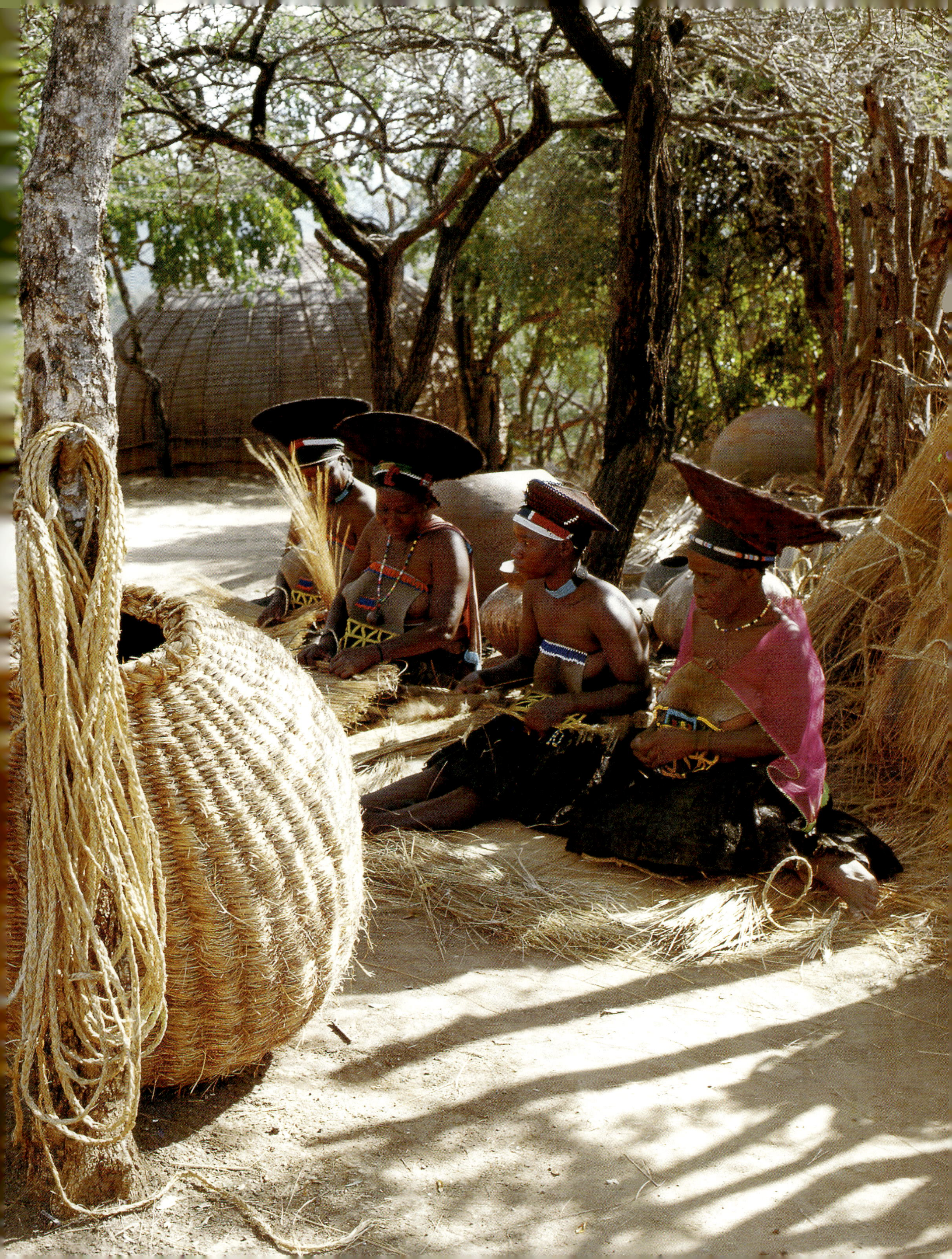

ABOVE AND TOP *These popular forms of beadwork are frequently made by young girls for their boyfriends.*

RIGHT *Beadwork is a craft at which Zulu women excel, though the origins of this craft among them is uncertain. Glass beads were first obtained through trade with European explorers, and would have been threaded onto animal gut. Today, however, cotton is used instead.*

53

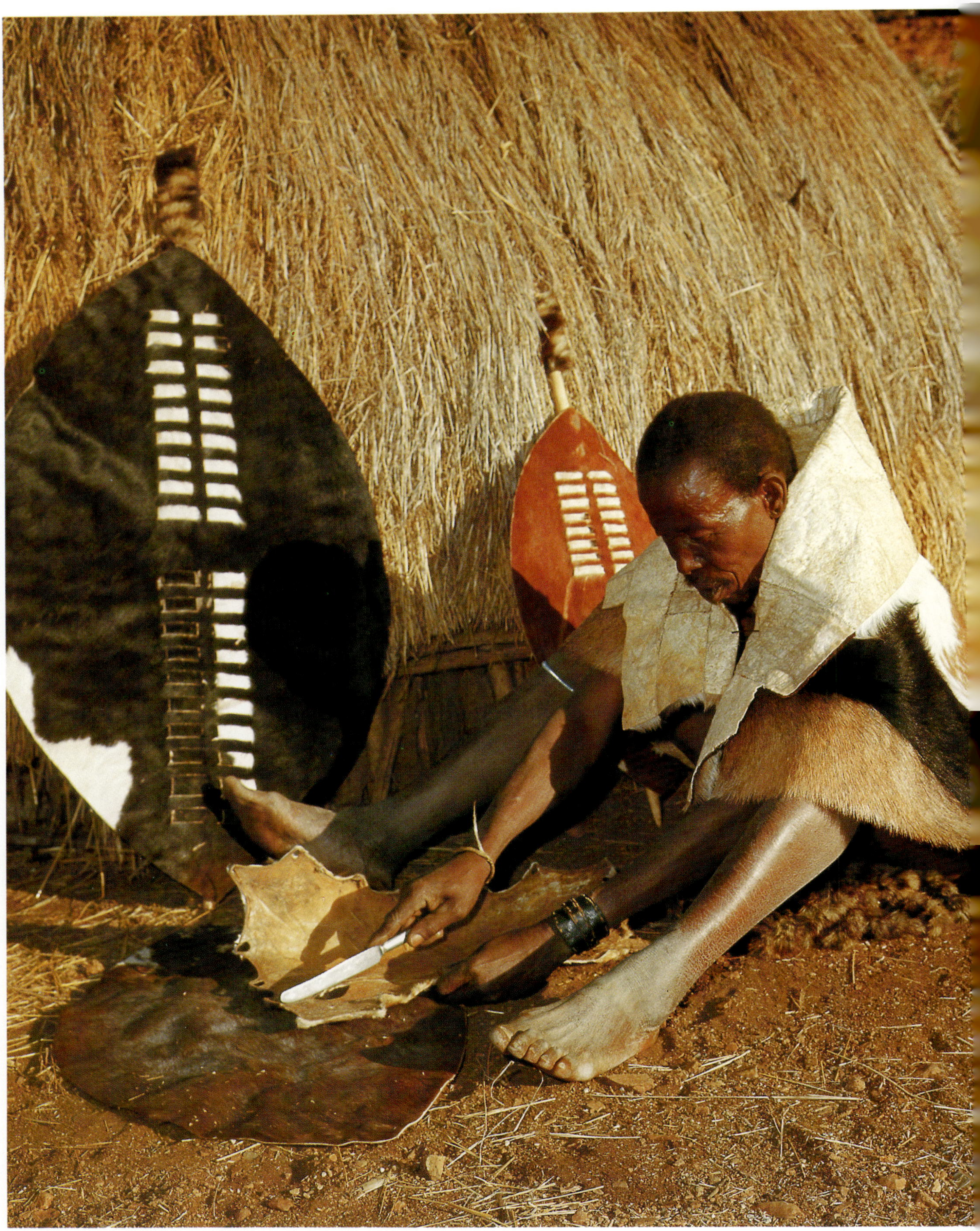

ABOVE *Goat skins are dried in the sun, either to serve as mats, or to make clothing and leather thongs.*

LEFT *The leather maker is something of a specialist in Zulu society, and much in demand. His products include not only shields, but also wraps – as can be seen from his own – sandals and various other useful articles.*

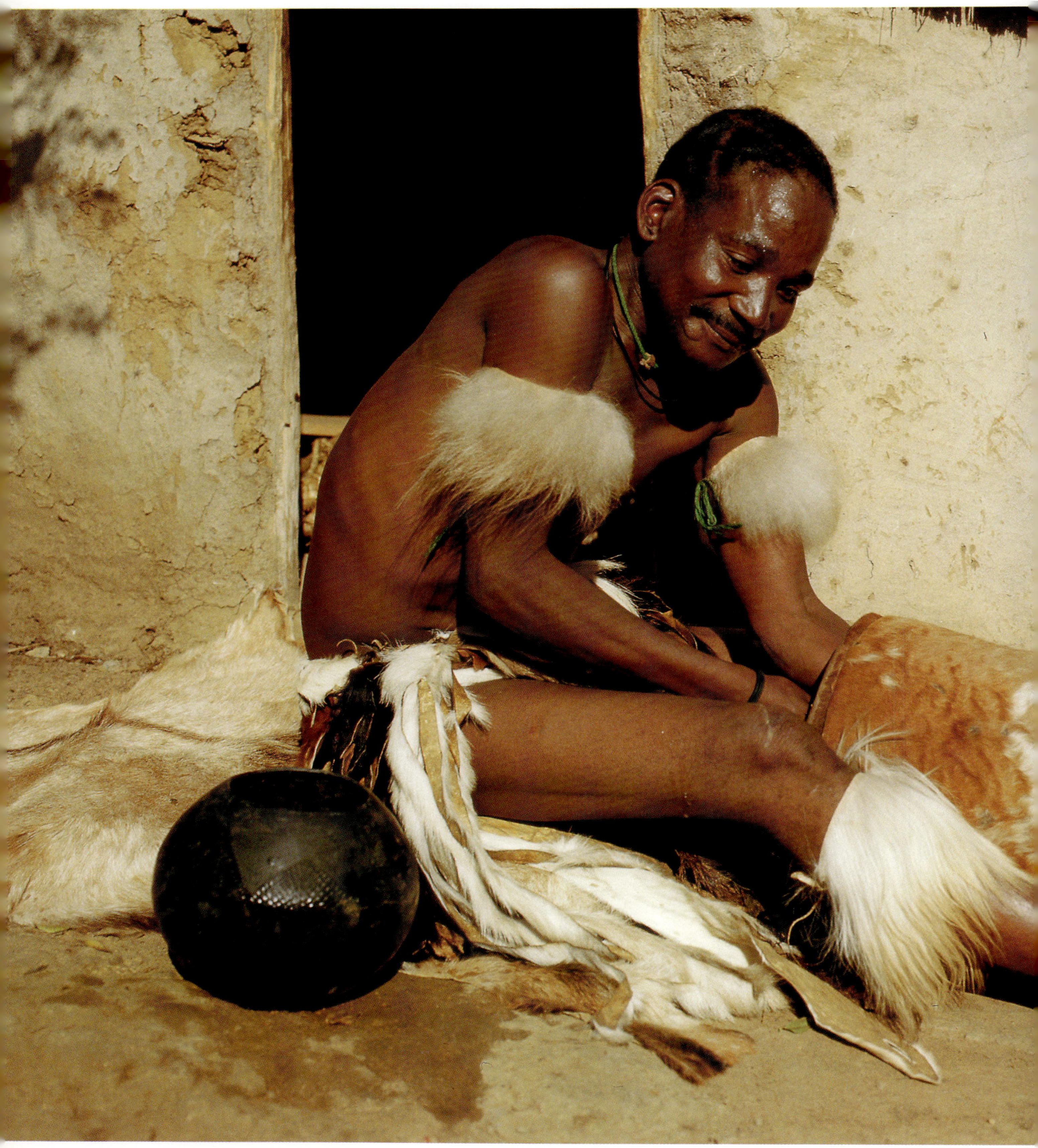

ABOVE AND OVERLEAF *Music and dance have long been important aspects of Zulu recreation, and the drum is a popular instrument. The oxhide drum skins tend to slacken in humid weather, so the owners place them beside a low fire to tighten them again.*

LEFT *This drum-like instrument has oxhide stretched across one side of the frame, while the other side remains open. A long, smooth stick is attached to the inside of the hide. The musician sits with the instrument between his legs, wets his fingers in a pot of water and pulls them along the stick, causing the hide to reverberate.*

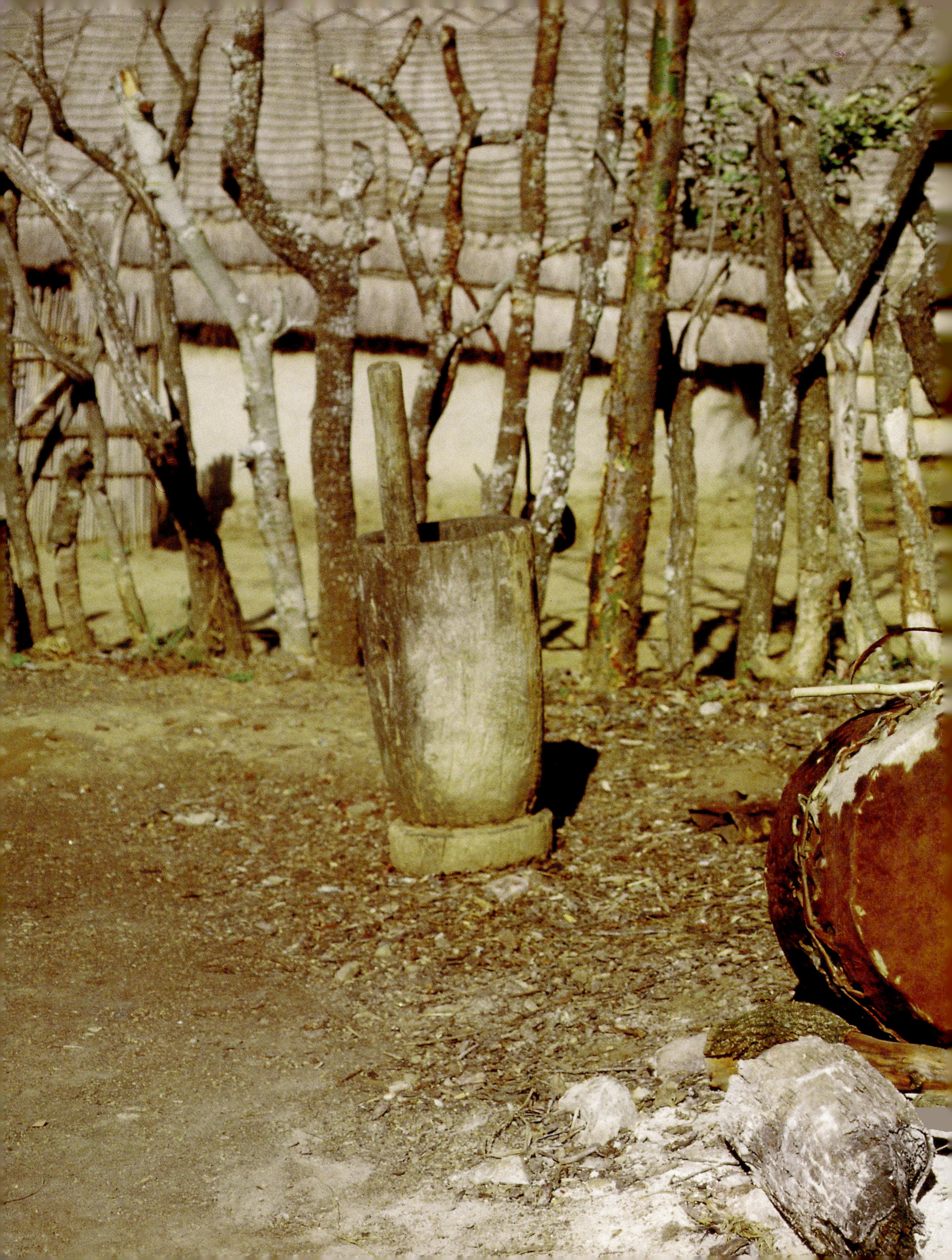

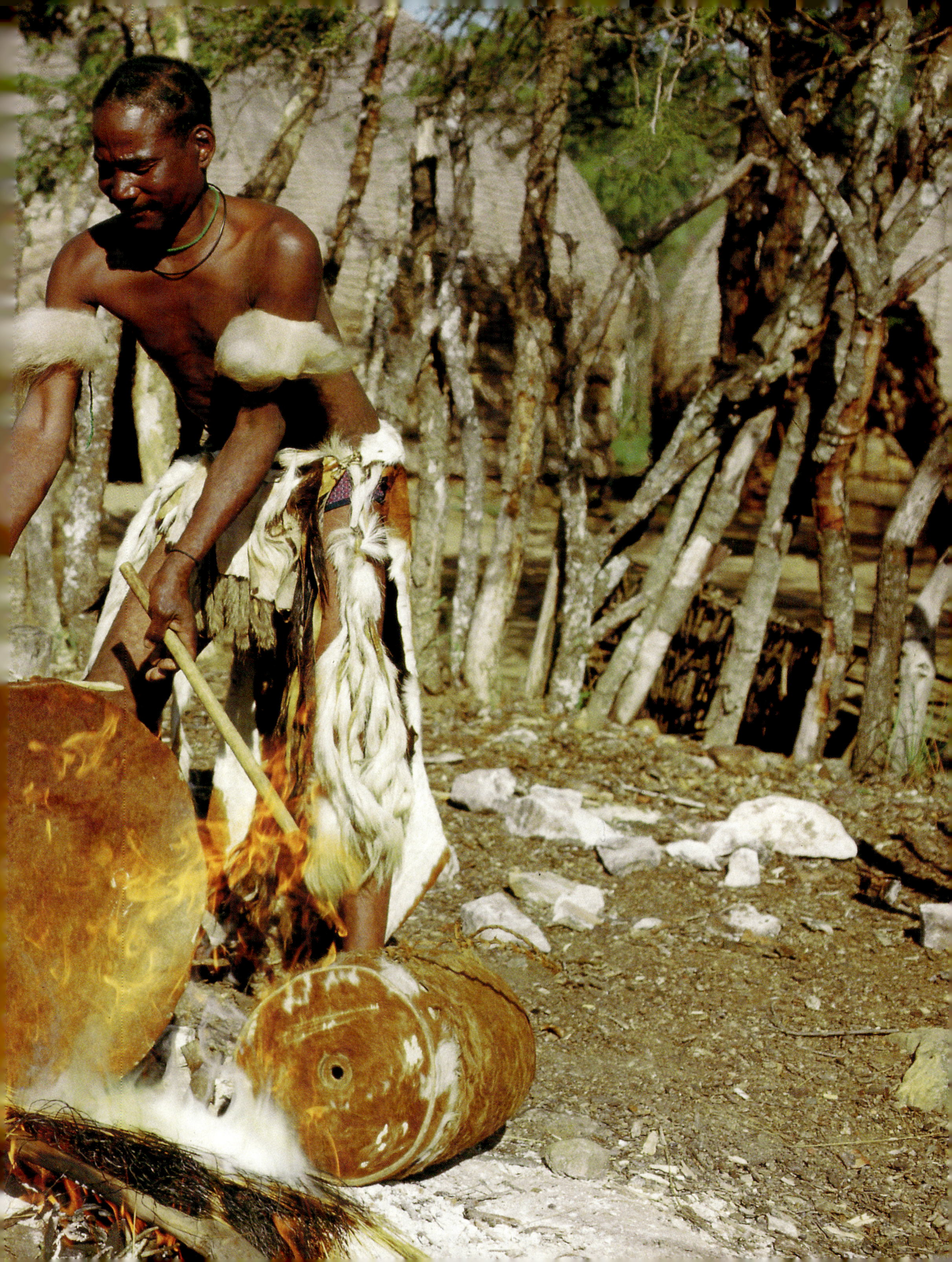

RIGHT *It is fairly common practice for the men of the rural black population of South Africa to migrate to the cities for a few years to work, mostly on the mines. Periodically, the mine organizations arrange 'mine dances', occasions for the labourers to show off their skills both as dancers and musicians, and these have become popular tourist attractions.*

LEFT *The* telonka *is a bull's horn, which an expert (using considerable lung power) blows to summon guests from distant regions to a wedding.*

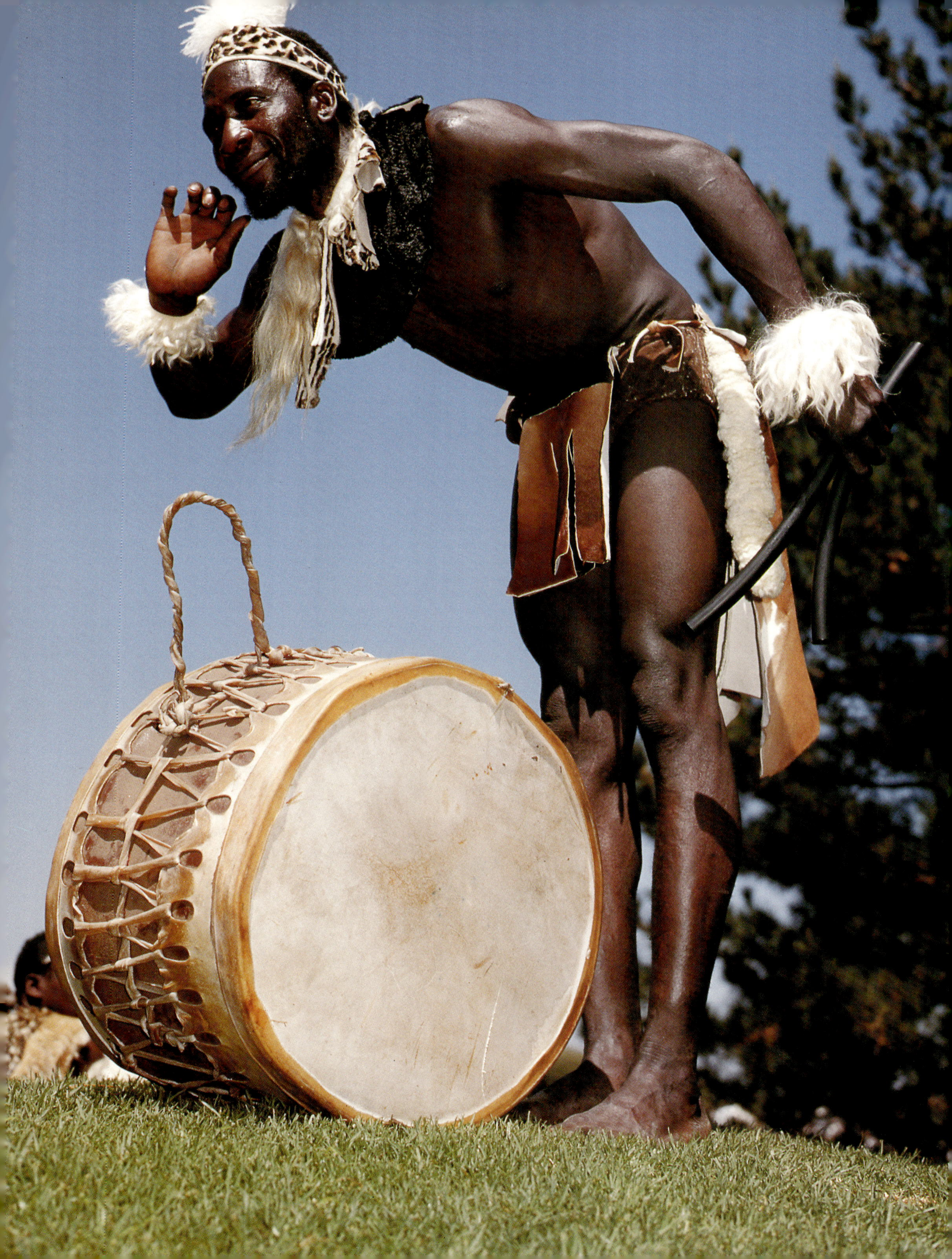

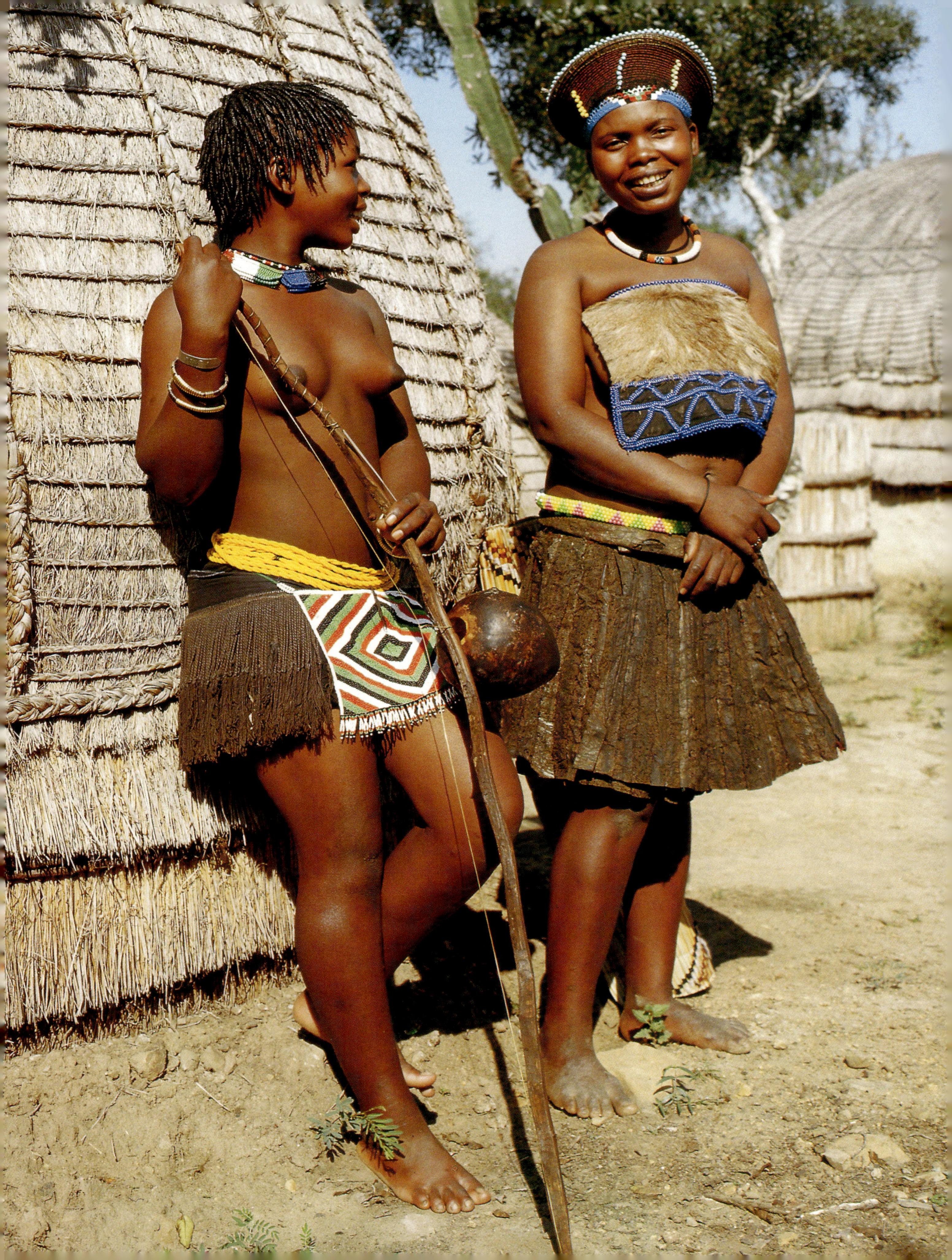

RIGHT *This young lady was adjudged the winner of a 'best-dressed woman' competition that took place among the Cele tribespeople at Dweshula. She was the youngest of six wives of a prominent local man.*

LEFT *The* **makhweyana** *is a single-stringed instrument, played by tapping the string with a small stick. The calabash is placed against the breast during playing, in order to provide resonance.*

ABOVE, RIGHT AND OVERLEAF
Dancing is a very popular pastime among the Zulu people, and they need little prompting to show off their considerable talent – not to mention physical fitness. The routines are highly structured, embodying the traditions and lore of the clans. The dances the men undertake invariably tend towards stylized battle movements, and shields and sticks are therefore part of the ceremonial regalia.

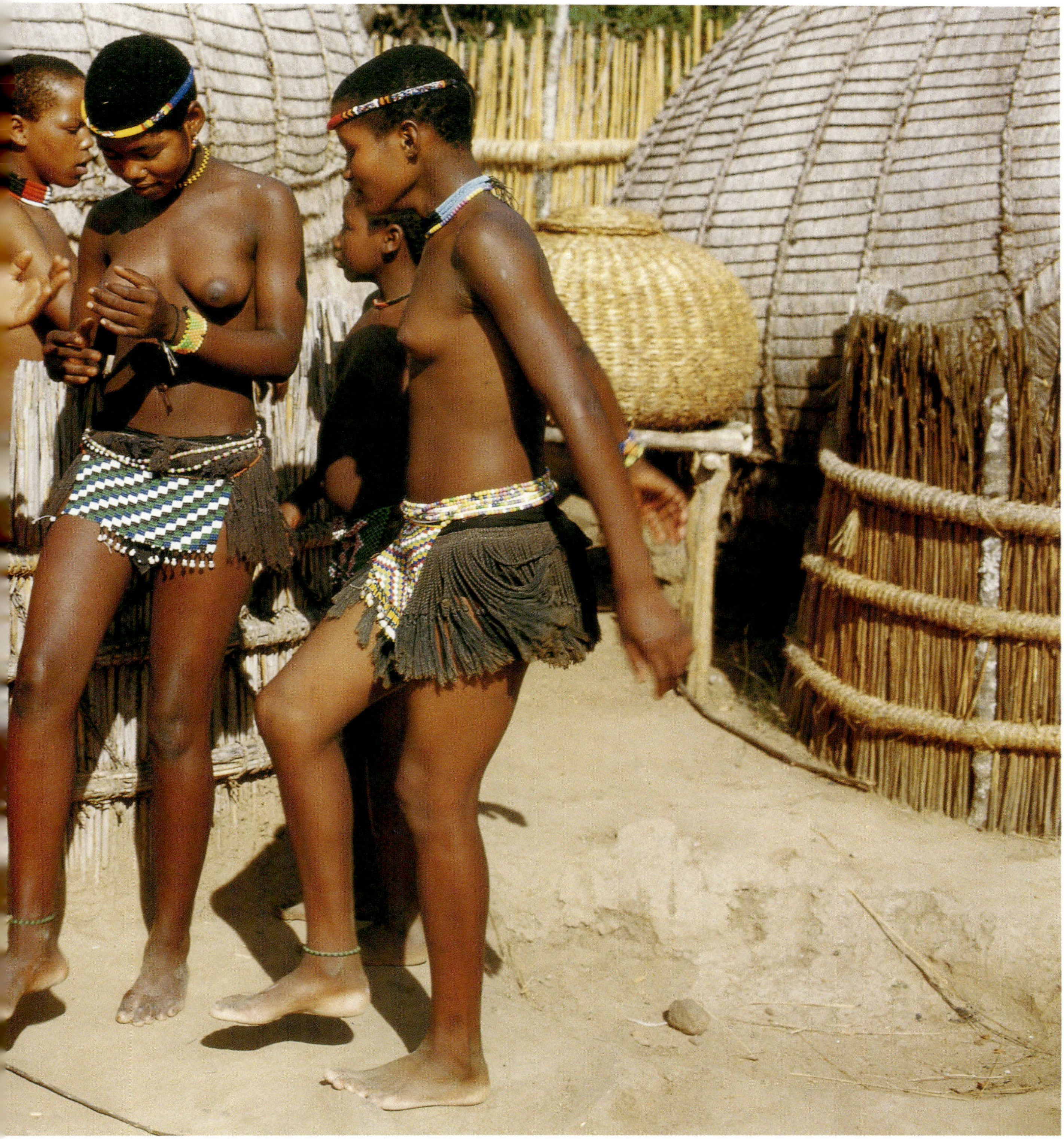

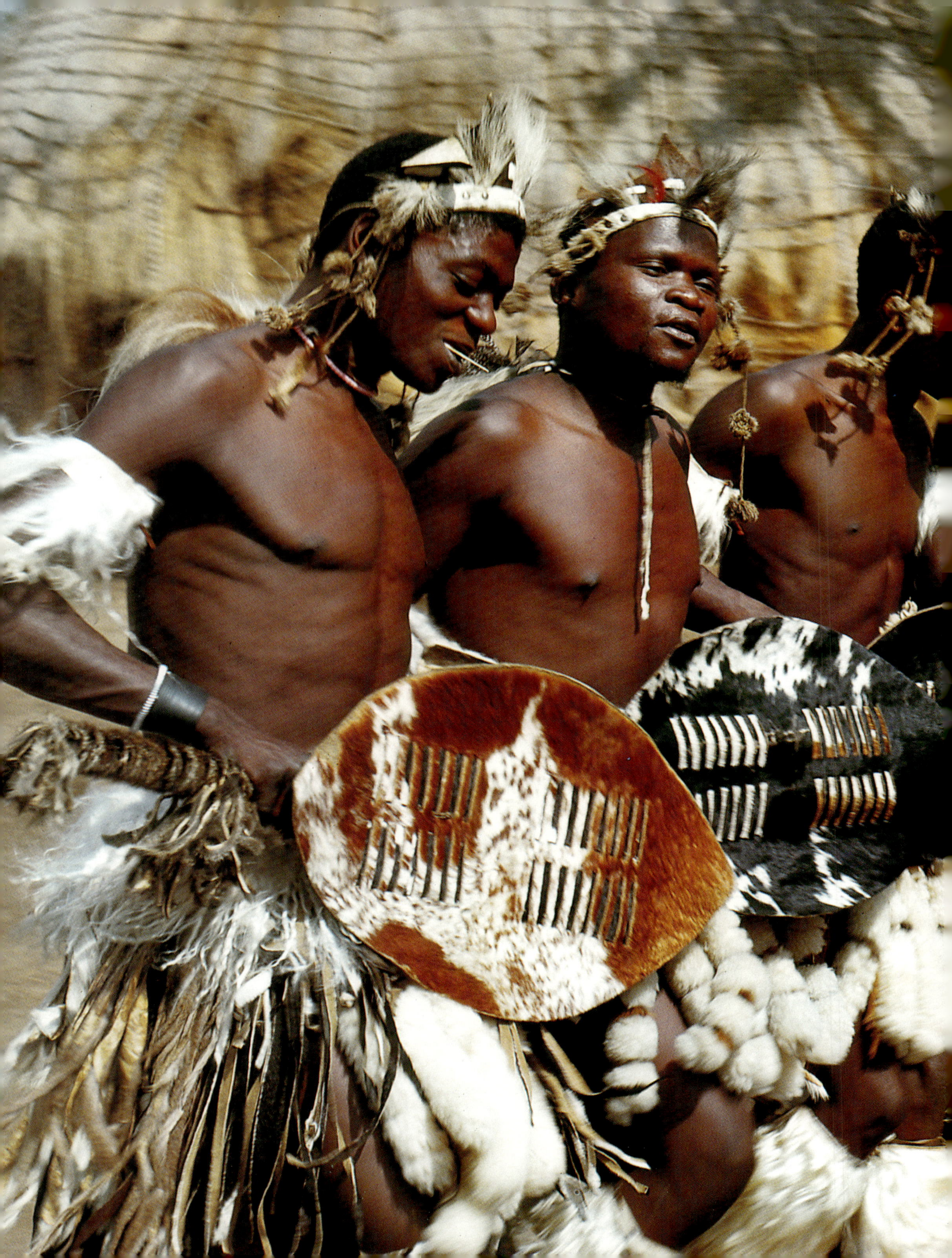

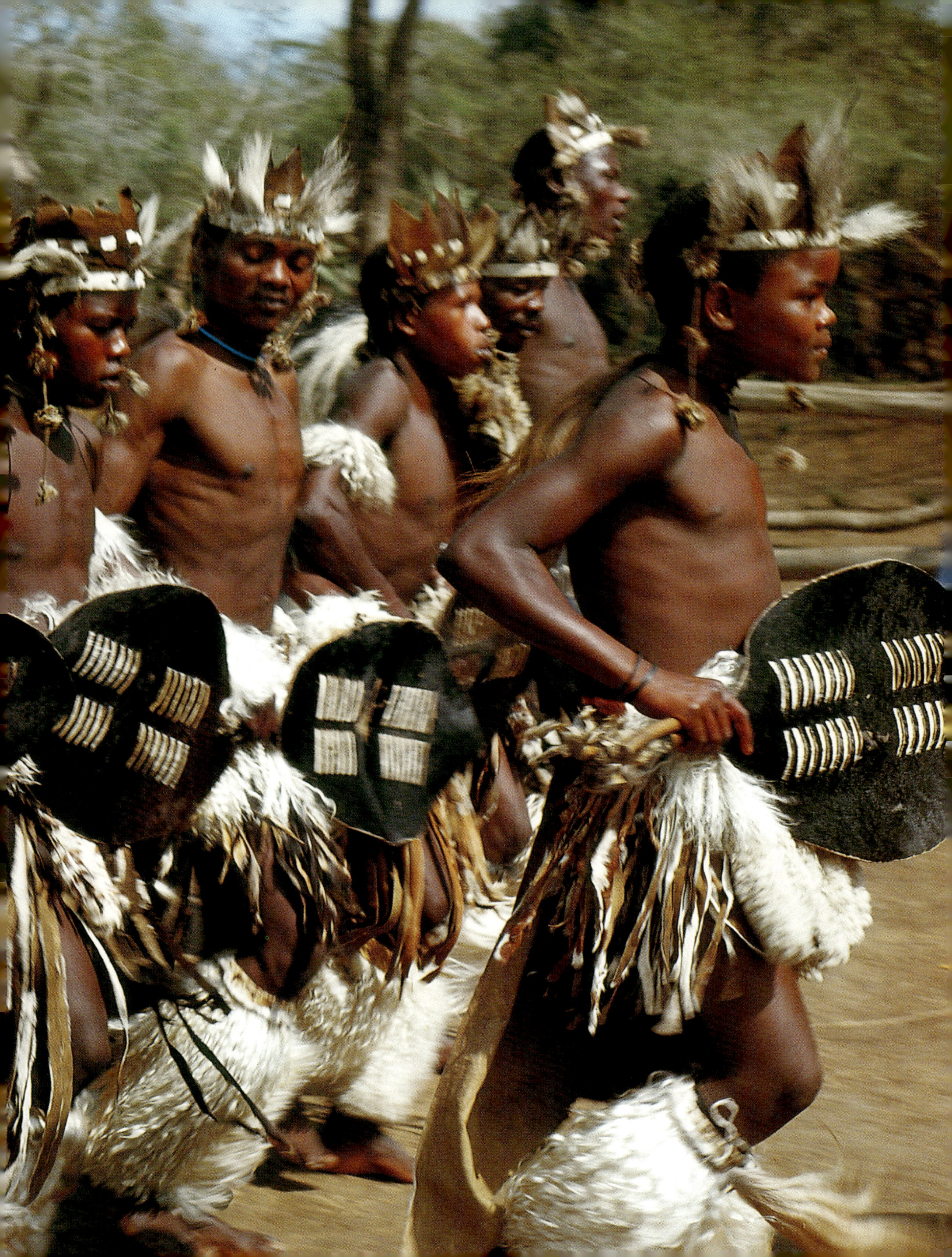

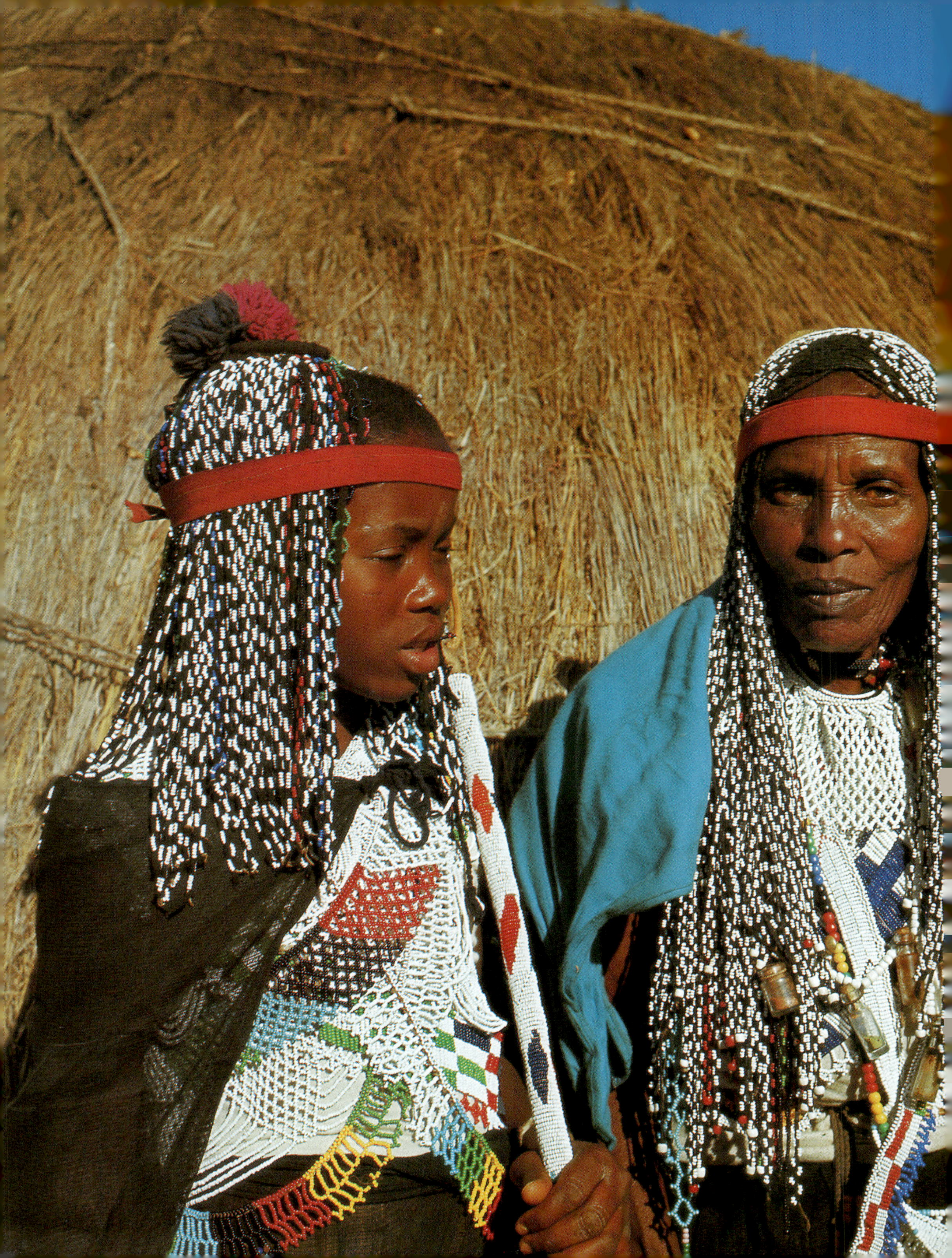

ABOVE **Sangoma**, *or diviners, are people of substantial power in traditional Zulu society, and have considerable influence even in the Westernized black urban communities. Here a diviner conducts a seance with two clients who wish to know the cause of certain problems.*

LEFT *These two* **sangoma** *are grandmother and 14-year-old grandson. Normally, a child in Zulu tribal society is expected to maintain a low profile and not assume any form of authority in adult company. This young boy was, however, already assuming the full authority of a diviner, and reputedly proving his merit among his people.*

ABOVE *The curing of ailments is an important part of a diviner's work, and the herbs and medicines used are often surprisingly effective. Here, a* sangoma *and a herbalist attend to a man with an aching back.*

ABOVE RIGHT *A tutor leads her pupils in a dance on the occasion of their induction into the* sangoma's *profession.*

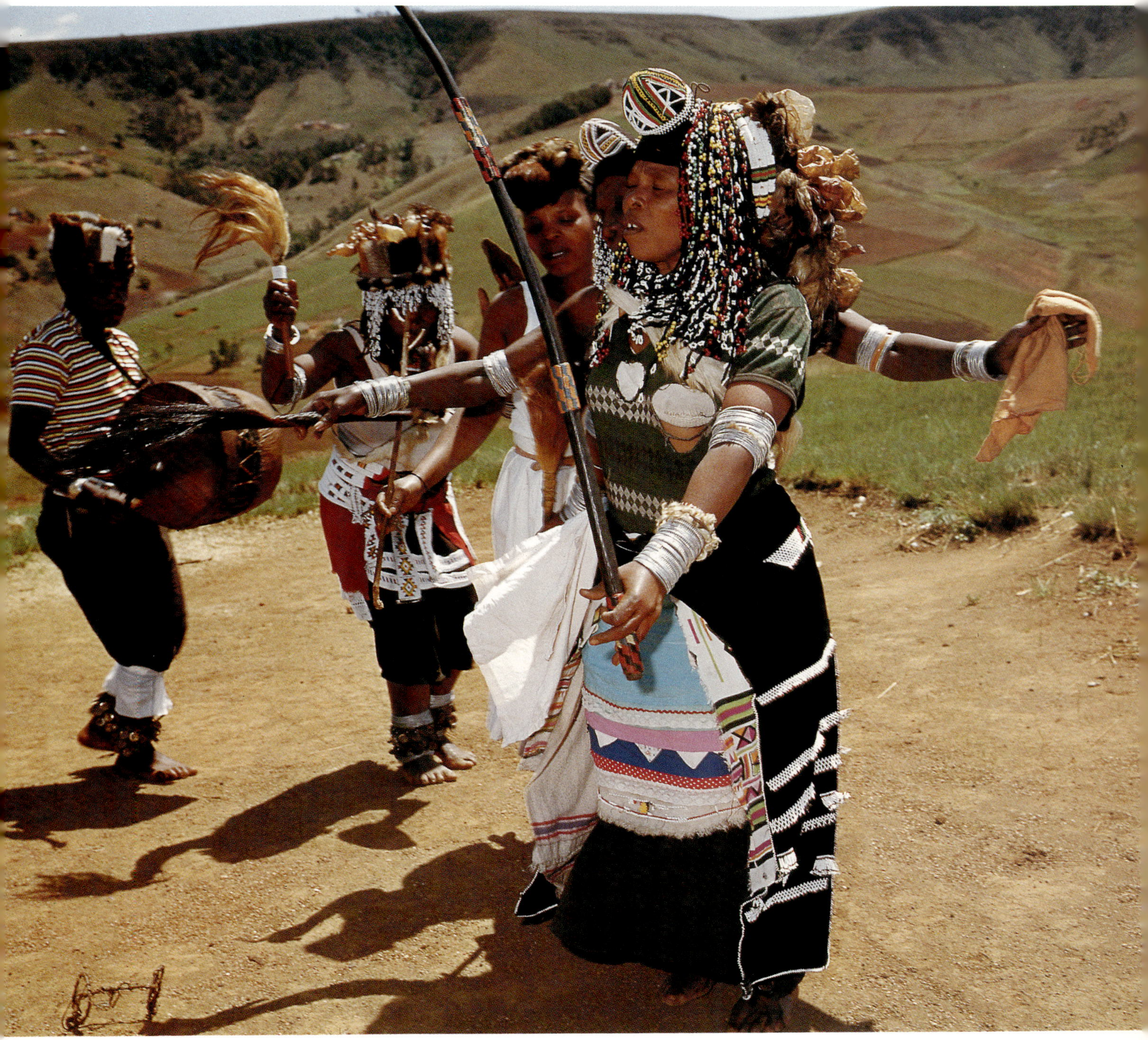

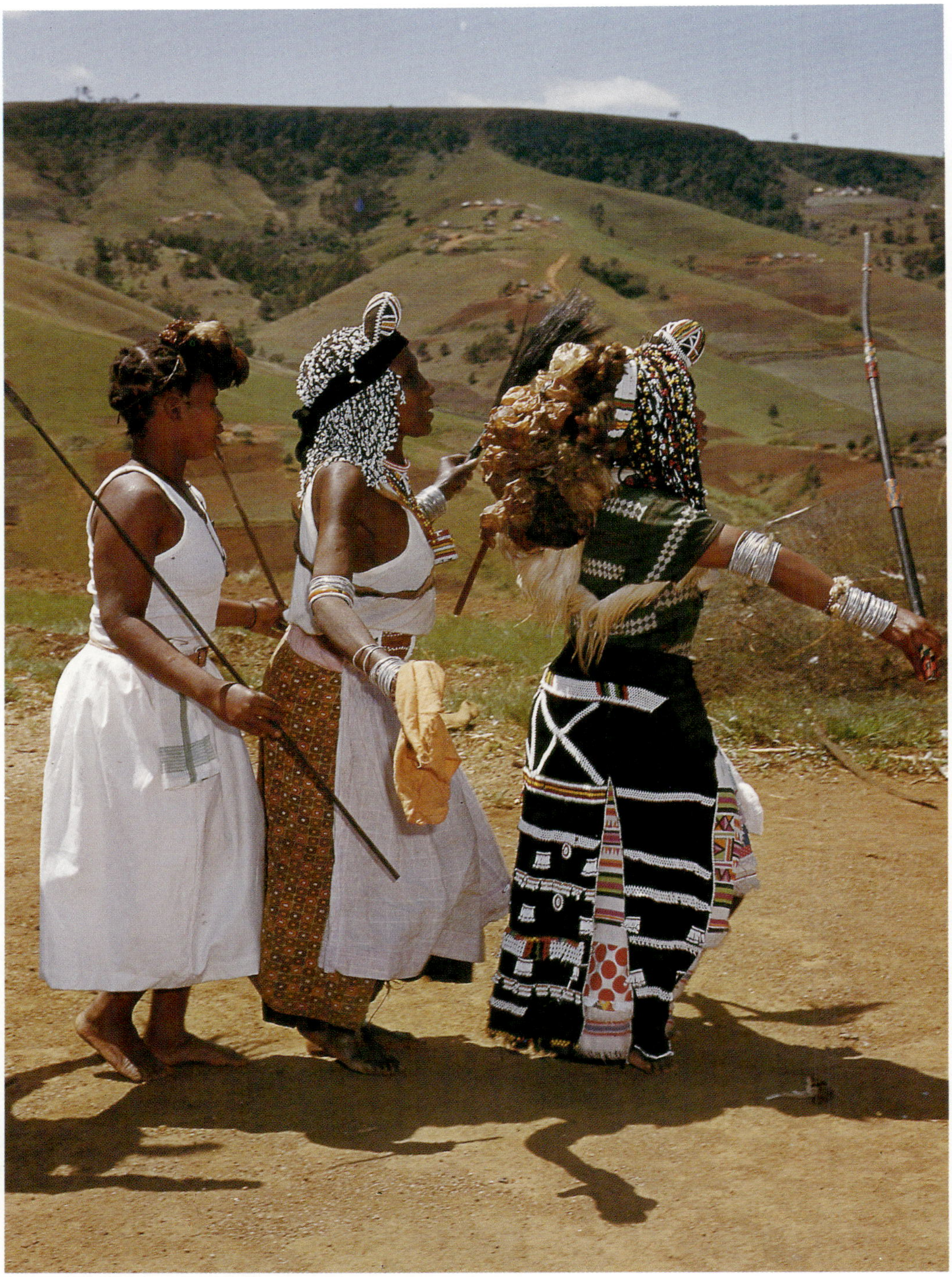

ABOVE *The dress of the* sangoma *tends to be very elaborate, a symbol of their status in Zulu society.*

ABOVE LEFT *The sjambok is often carried by diviners as a symbol of authority. The common Western name for* sangoma *is 'witch doctor', but this term is confusing, as the Zulu make clear distinctions between* sangoma, *who are diviners and healers, and witches, who are evil beings.*

ABOVE *Diviners offer up a goat as a sacrifice to the ancestral spirits at a seance at Msinga. For this purpose, the animal is killed by driving a spear through the base of the neck and into the heart.*

RIGHT *An old blacksmith beats out a new spear on a rock anvil at Graham Stewart's guest farm at Nkwalini, a place where the traditional Zulu life style can still be seen.*

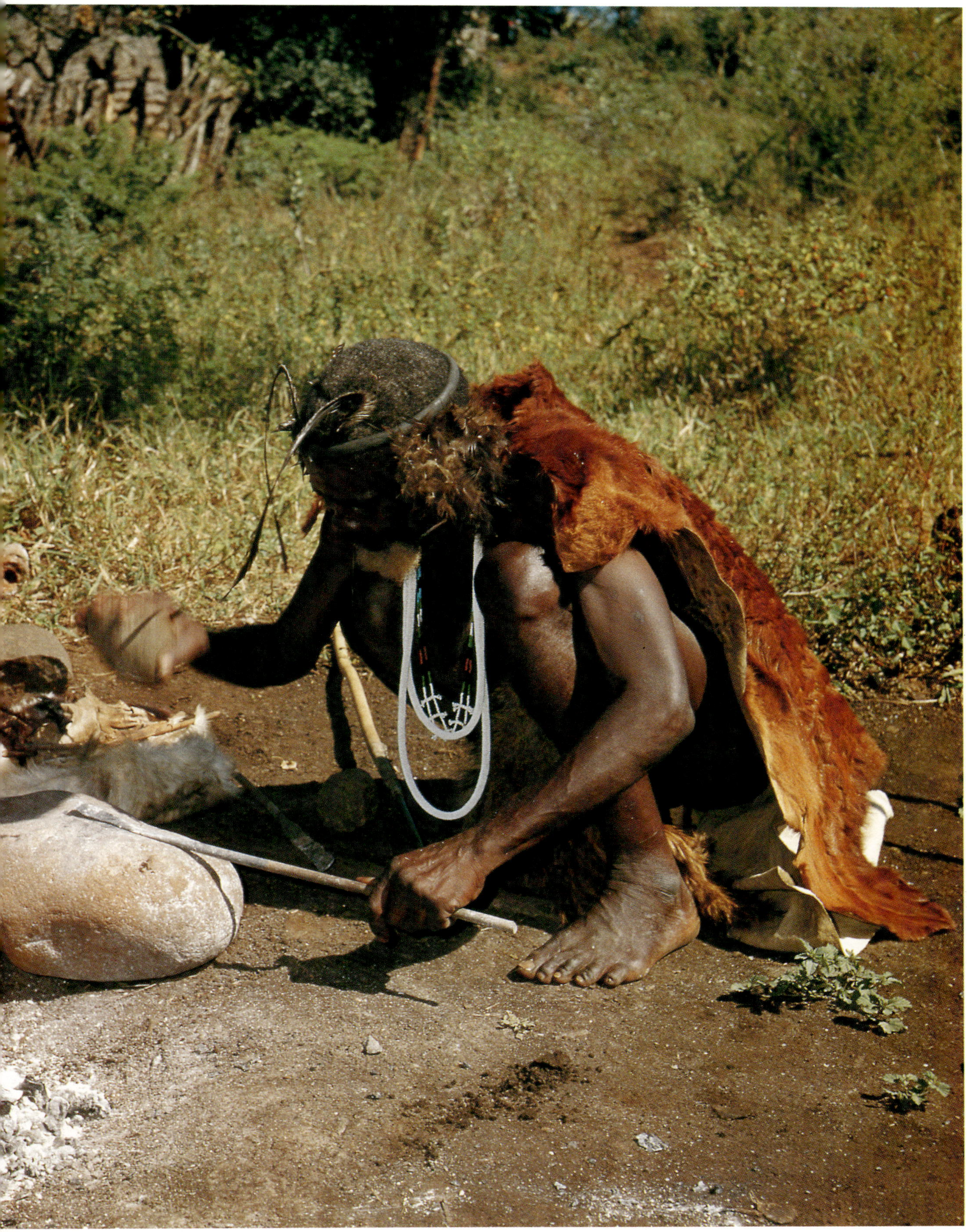

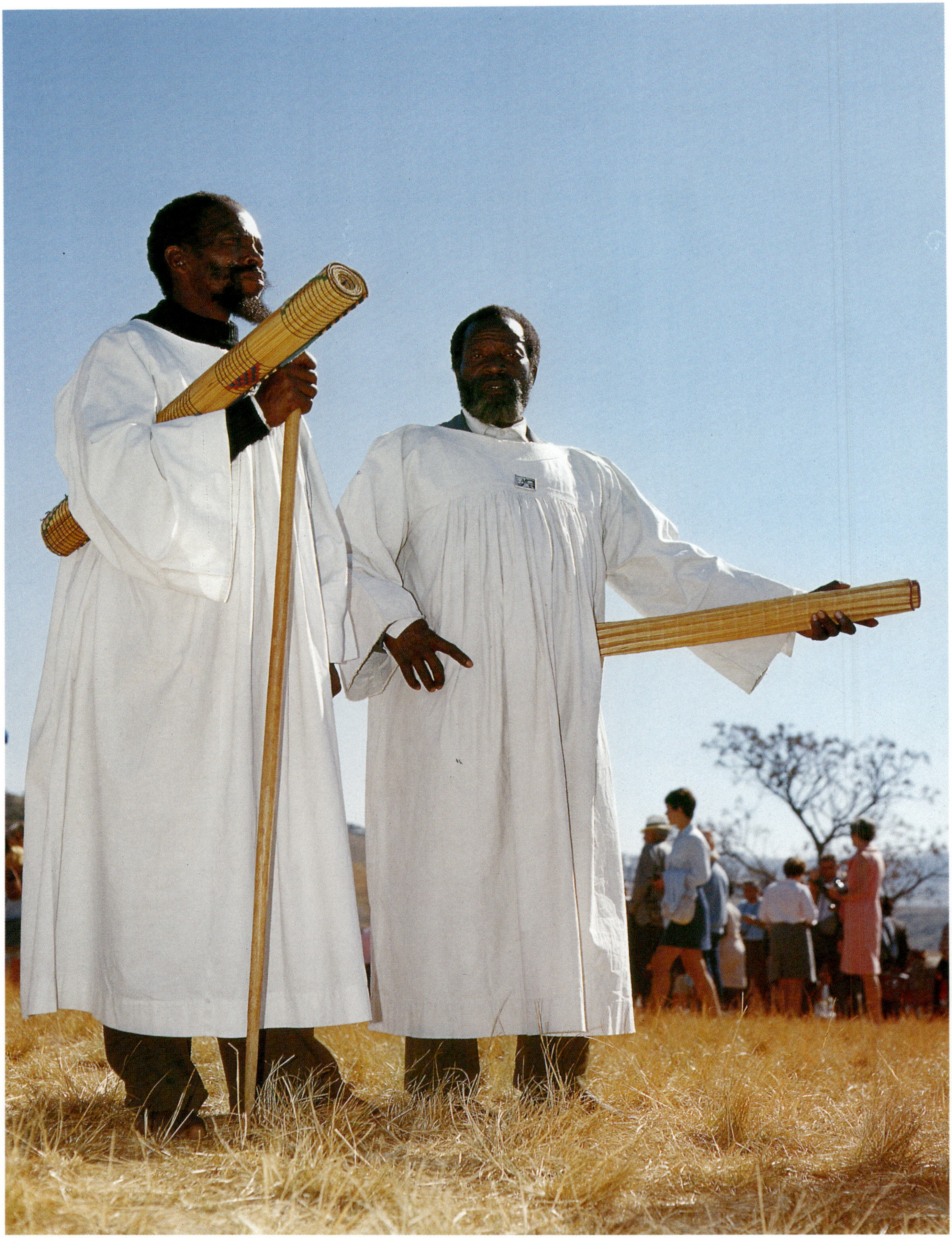

ABOVE *Although ancestor worship is the traditional Zulu religion, Christianity has gained considerable ground in recent years. One of the more popular denominations was founded by a prophet named Shembe. Here, a priest presides over a religious ceremony at Ekuphakumeni in 1969.*

LEFT *Zulu church officers, cutting impressive figures in their white robes, attend a Shembe religious ceremony.*

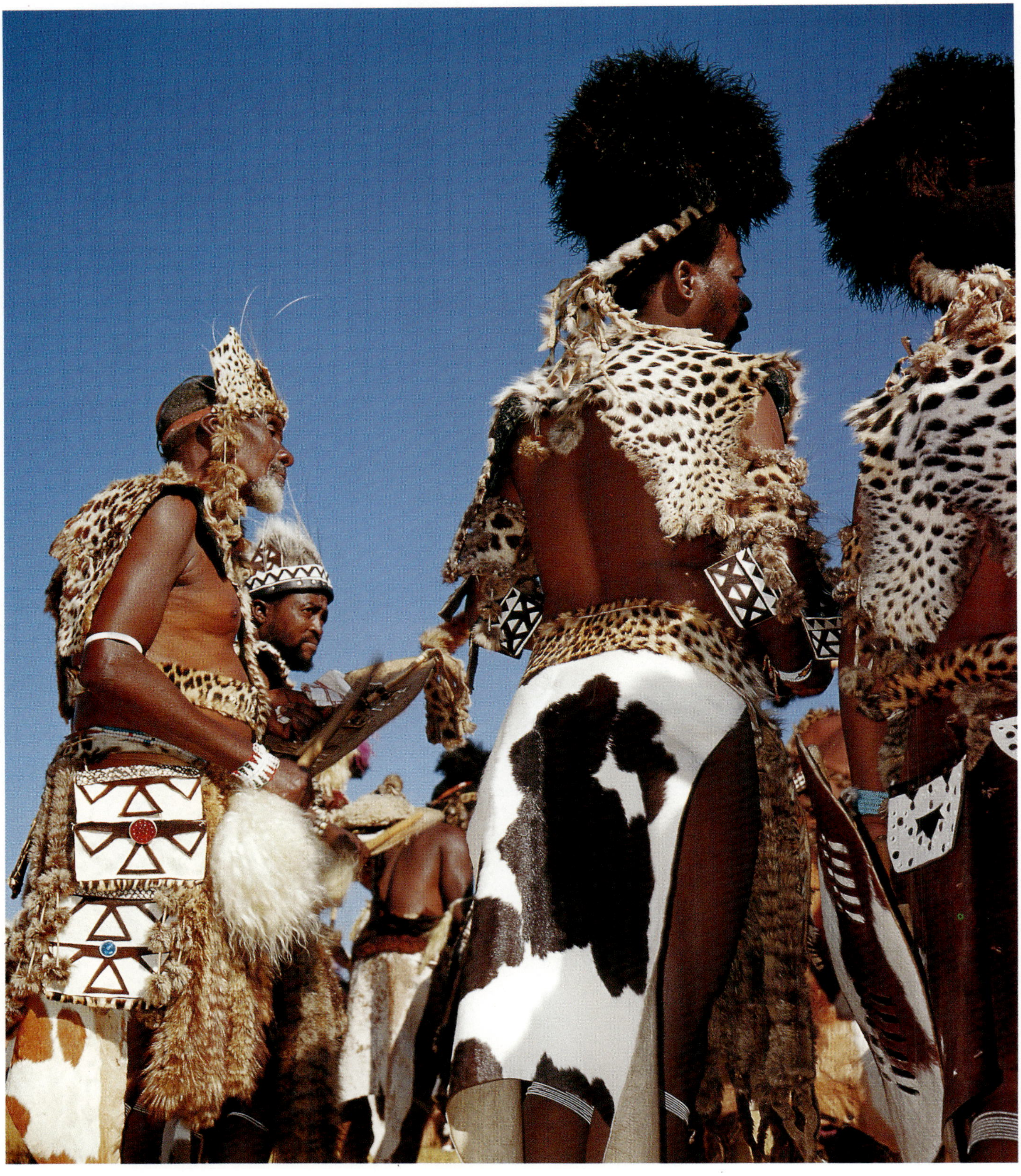

Unlike many missionaries of old, who insisted on the discarding of national dress, Shembe encouraged the wearing of traditional regalia at ceremonial occasions. Such occasions involve dancing and singing accompanied by drums and trumpets, and are indeed awe-inspiring events.

The Zulu traditionally follow the ancestor cult, an important aspect of which is the offering up of cattle to the ancestors. When an ox is killed, its horns are placed on the thatched roof of the home for all passers by to see. These horns point upwards 'that all may know the family have not forgotten their fathers'. If an animal is killed 'just because the family want meat' its horns are pointed downwards.